Writing Around in Cars

By Ron Kretschmer

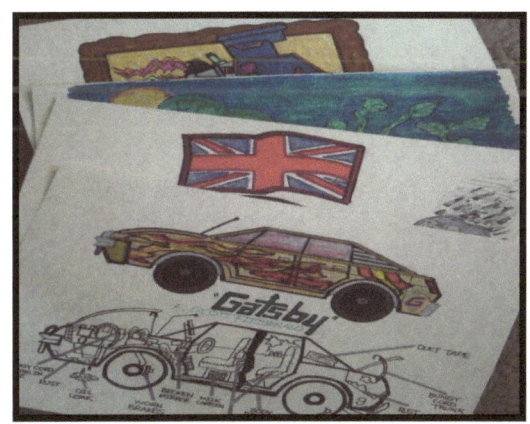

"Writing Around in Cars"
Copyright 2018 Ron Kretschmer

Hosmer Press, 2018
Tacoma, WA

All copy and illustrations are property of Ron Kretschmer and can not be used or reproduced without permission.

Writing Around in Cars is a dumb title made out of a dumb pun. I admit it. This is unlike the other books I have written in that it is mostly illustrations and has no plot. It started out as a few random drawings I made when I had other things to do but didn't feel like doing them on account that I was procrastinating. I ended up procrastinating even more as new ideas for vehicles inspired by my favorite books and authors invaded my imagination. At the very least, this is a better use of my drawing and painting. I was running out of wall space for the canvas works I had been creating during my epic bouts of procrastination, so I needed to find projects that could be preserved without having to buy a whole new building to house them.

These vehicles are not the actual cars that the authors drove (I believe that Charles Dickens drove a Hyundai). The illustrations represent what those fabled writers may have driven if they were able to put together automobiles based on either their works or their personality. Some of them get more than one car. It isn't fair to the other guys, but some just warrant an extra because I like them more. William Shakespeare not only receives multiple cars in this book, but he also finds his way into the company of the esteemed novelists despite actually being a playwright. I also included a car based on one of my own novels *(Tim Buck)*, which is somewhat arrogant on my part considering that everyone else in the book is a writer of great renown and I am merely of very casual renown. It only seems somewhat arrogant because it is. Sorry for that...kind of.

Life is short; live it well.
Ron Kretschmer

For Melissa who loves classics.

Table of contents:

F. Scott Fitzgerald
Mary Shelley
Daniel Defoe
L. Frank Baum
Leo Tolstoy
Oscar Wilde
Jules Verne
Ray Bradbury
Alexandre Dumas
H.G. Wells
Ron Kretschmer
William Shakespeare
Charles Dickens
Kurt Vonnegut Jr.
Herman Melville
Edgar Allan Poe
Rudyard Kipling
Sir Arthur Conan Doyle

F. Scott Fitzgerald

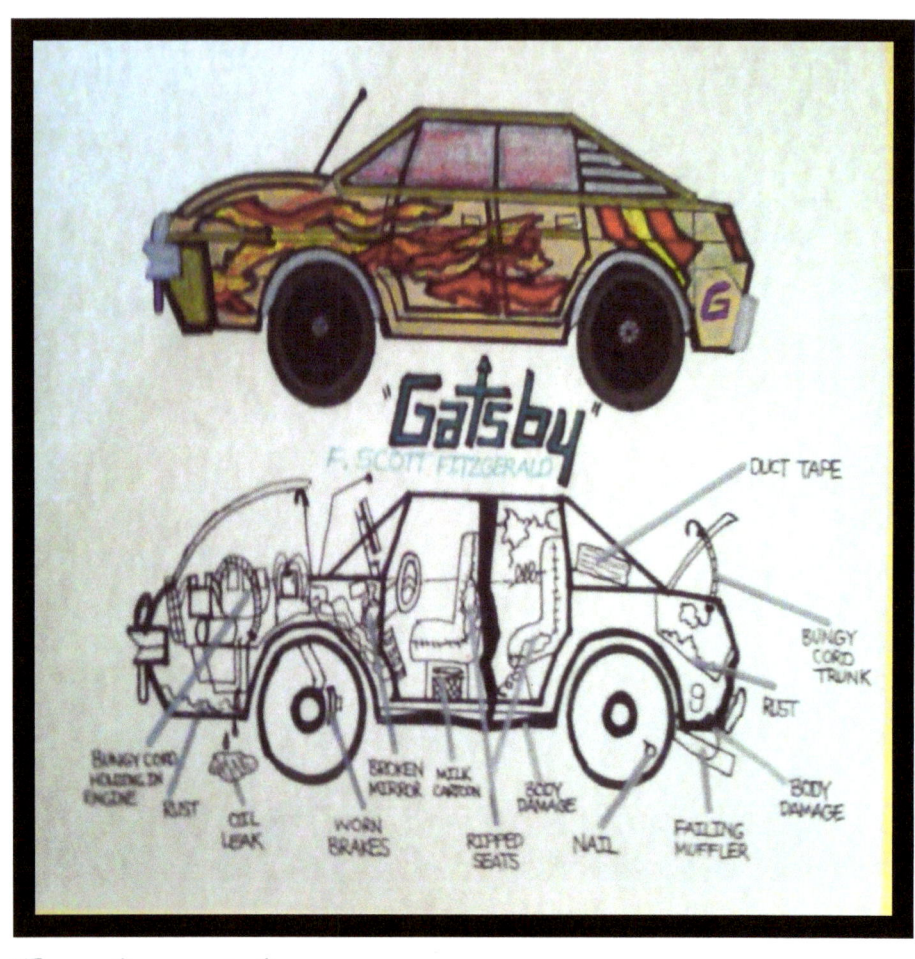

THE GREAT GATSBY

Mary Shelley

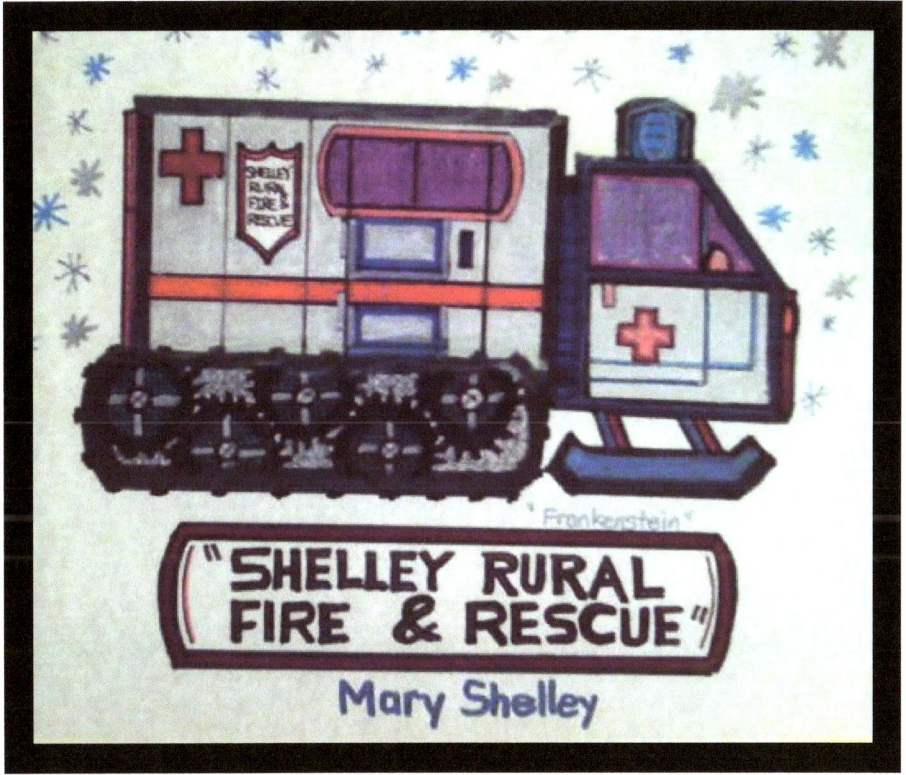

Frankenstein

Daniel Defoe

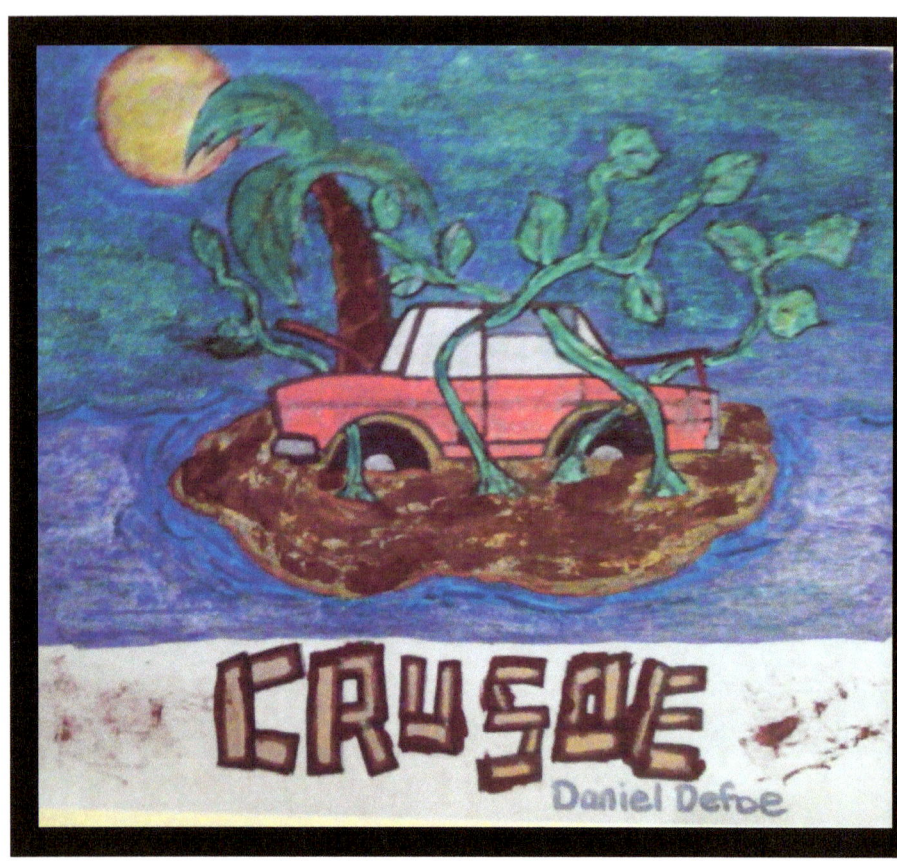

Robinson Crusoe

L. Frank Baum

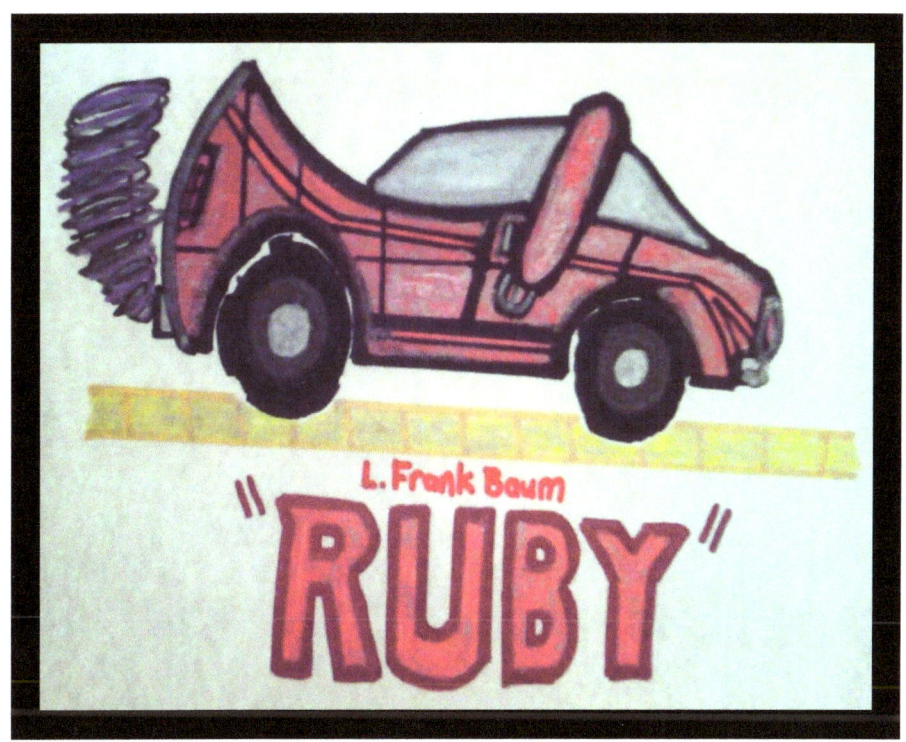

The Wizard of Oz

Leo Tolstoy

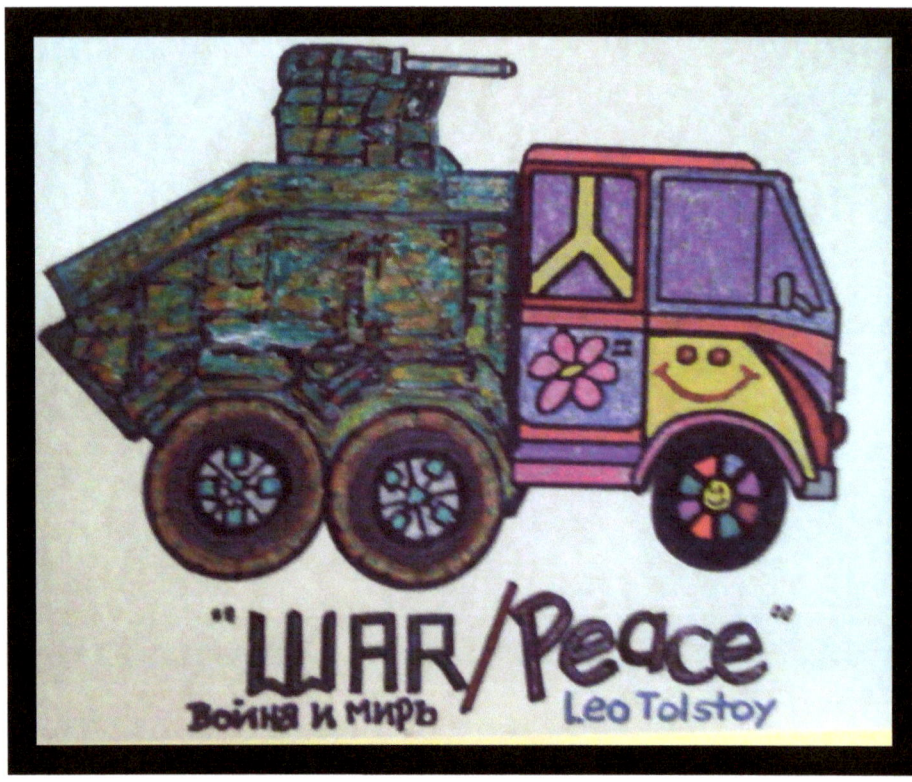

War and Peace
Война и мир

Oscar Wilde

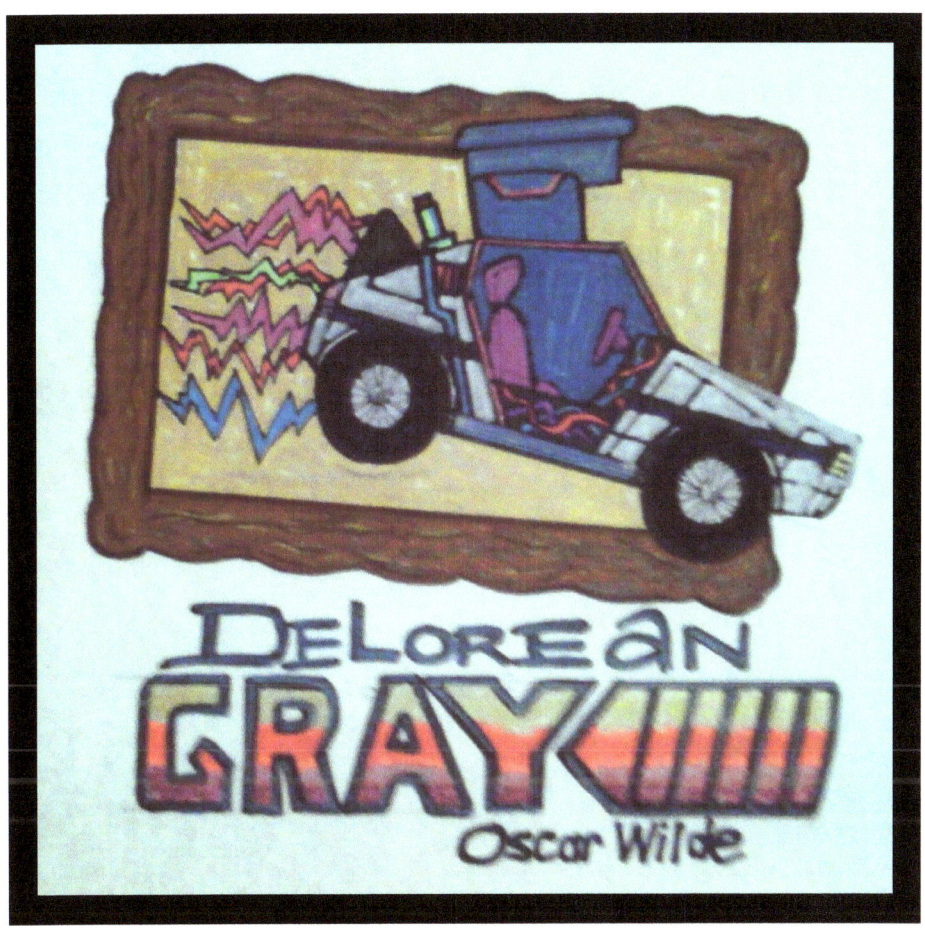

The Portrait of Dorian Gray

Jules Verne

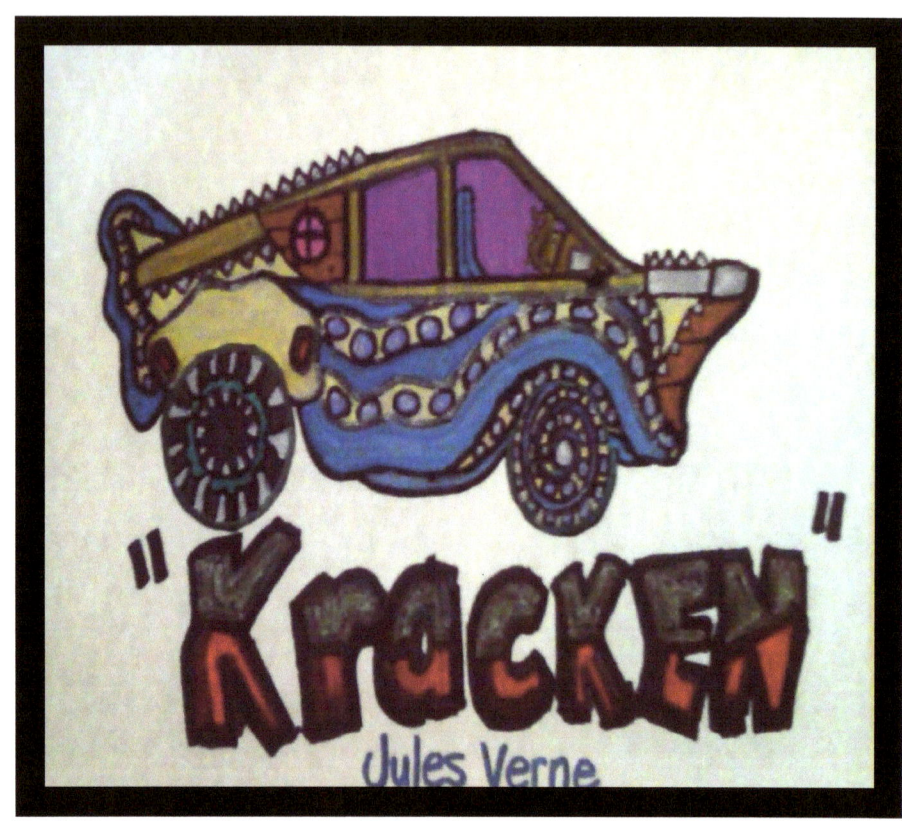

20,000 Leagues Under the Sea

Ray Bradbury

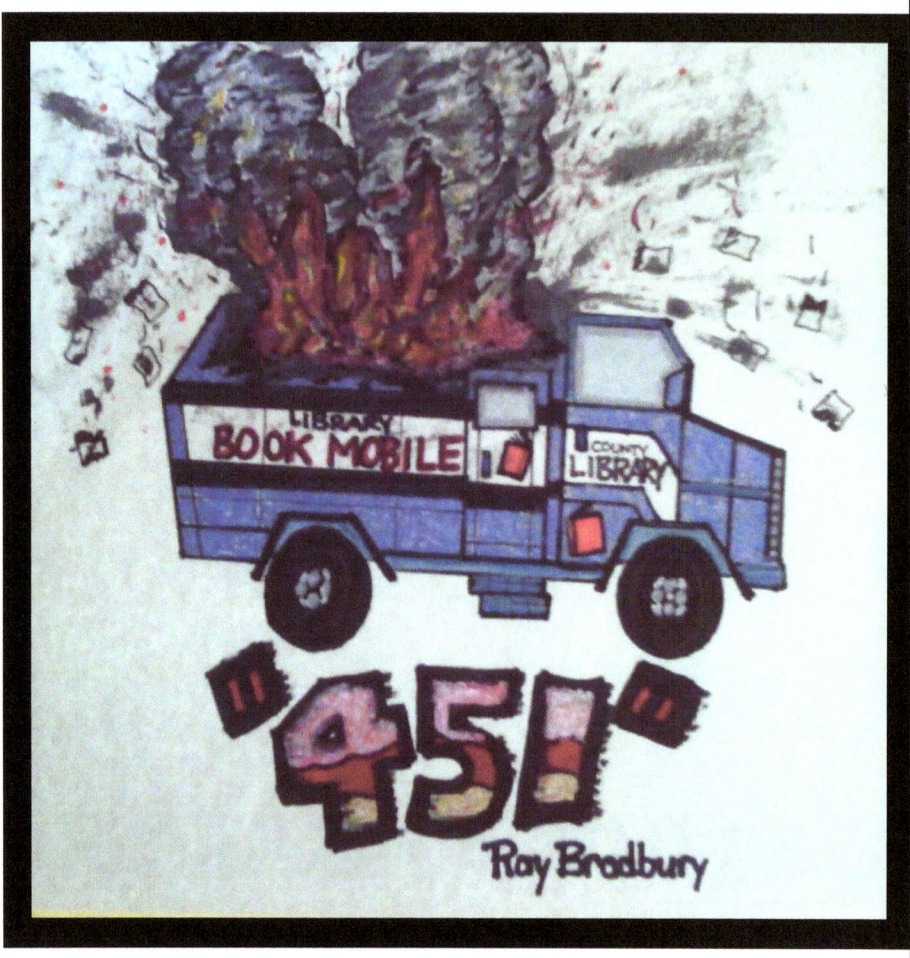

Fahrenheit 451

Alexandre Dumas

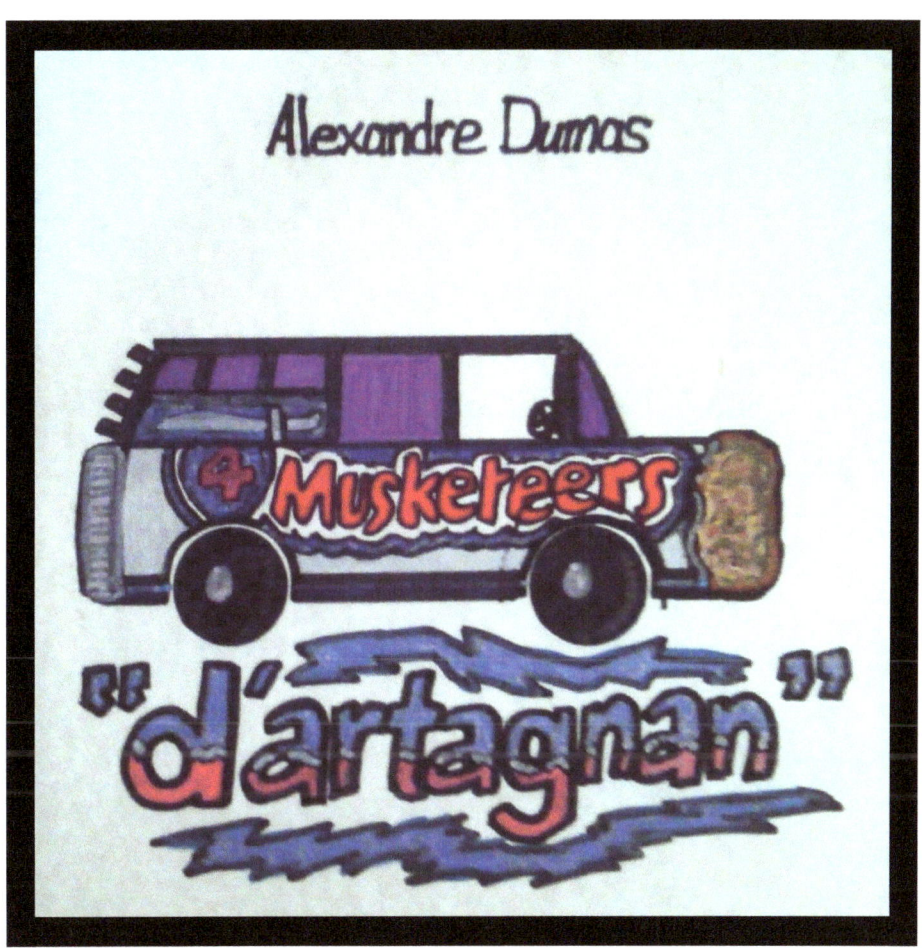

The Three Musketeers

H.G. WELLS — THE INVISIBLE MAN, THE TIME MACHINE

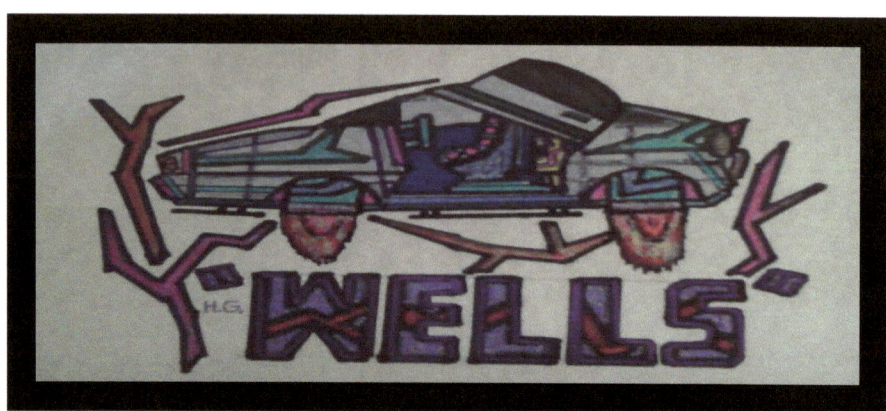

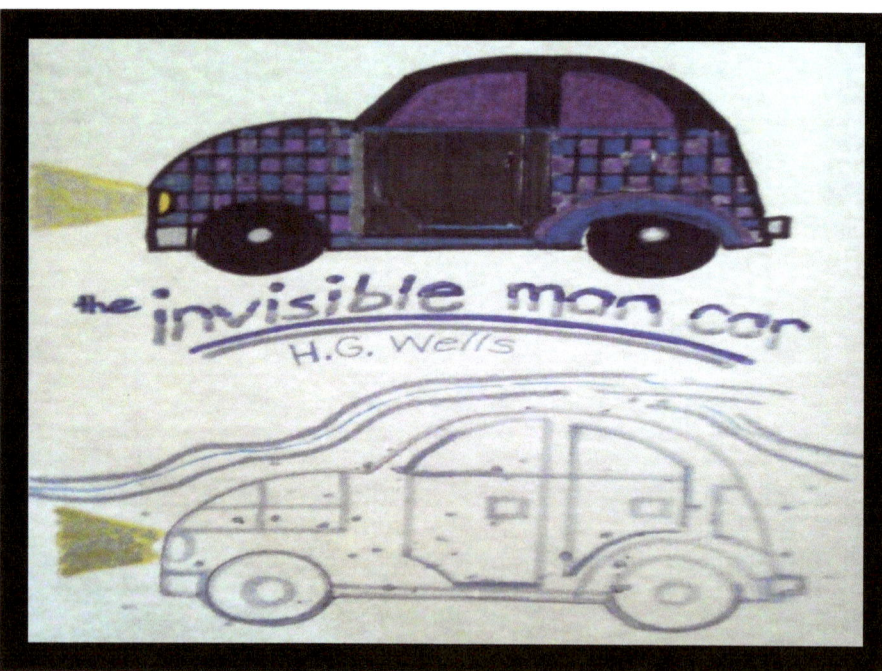

Ron kretschmer

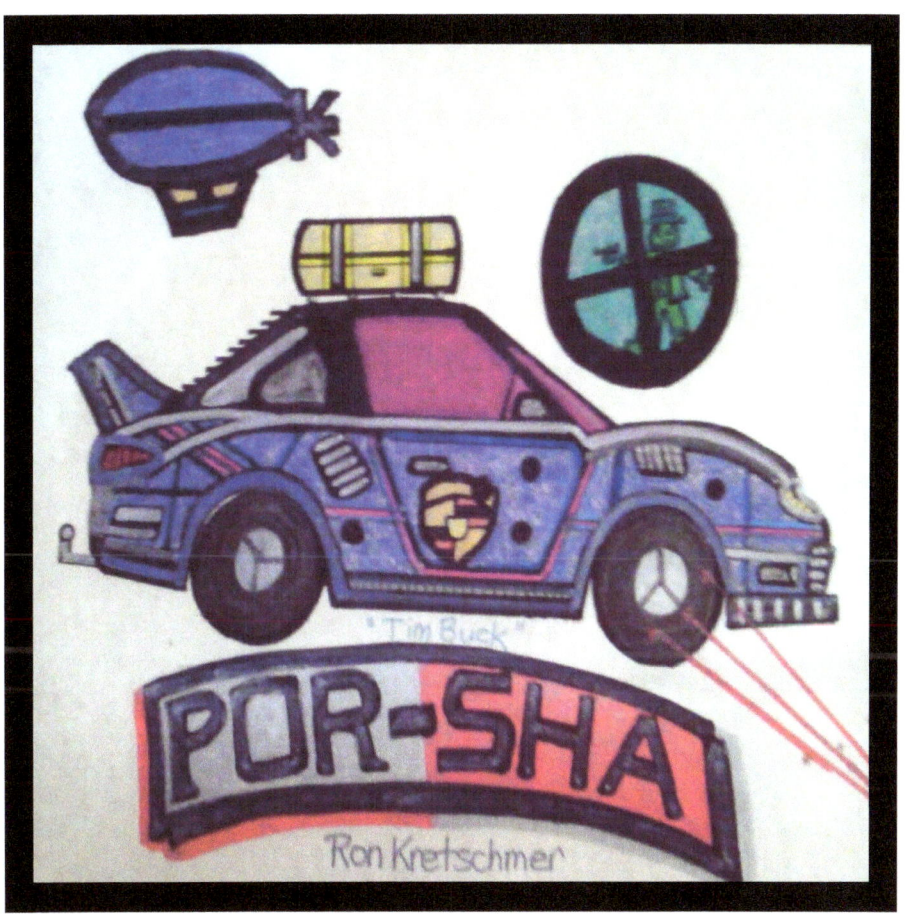

Tim buck

William Shakespeare – *Hamlet*

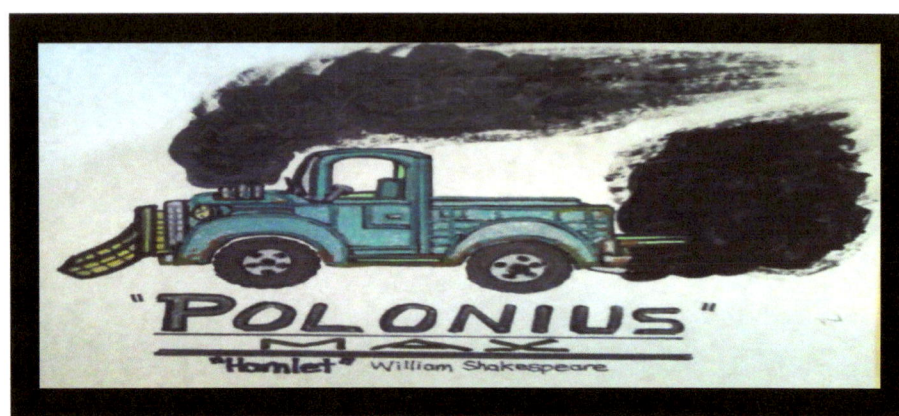

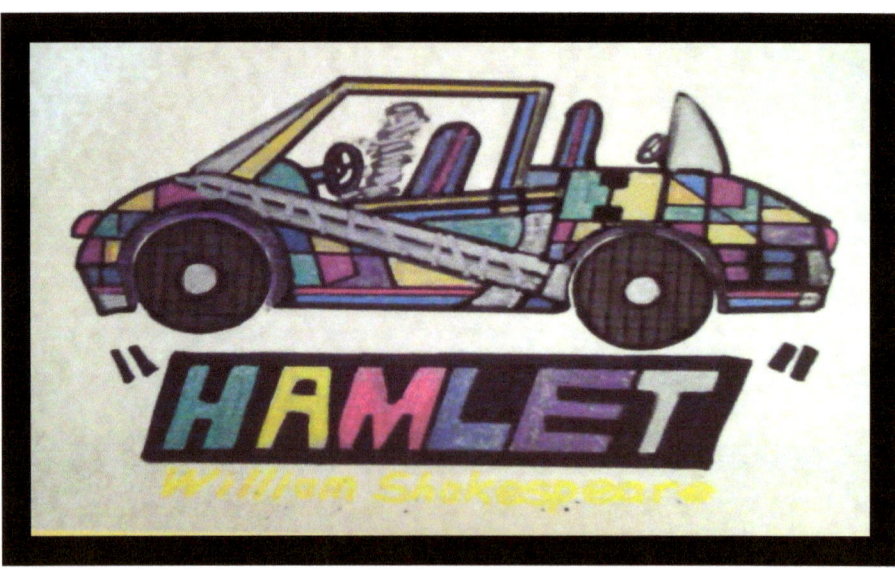

Charles dickens

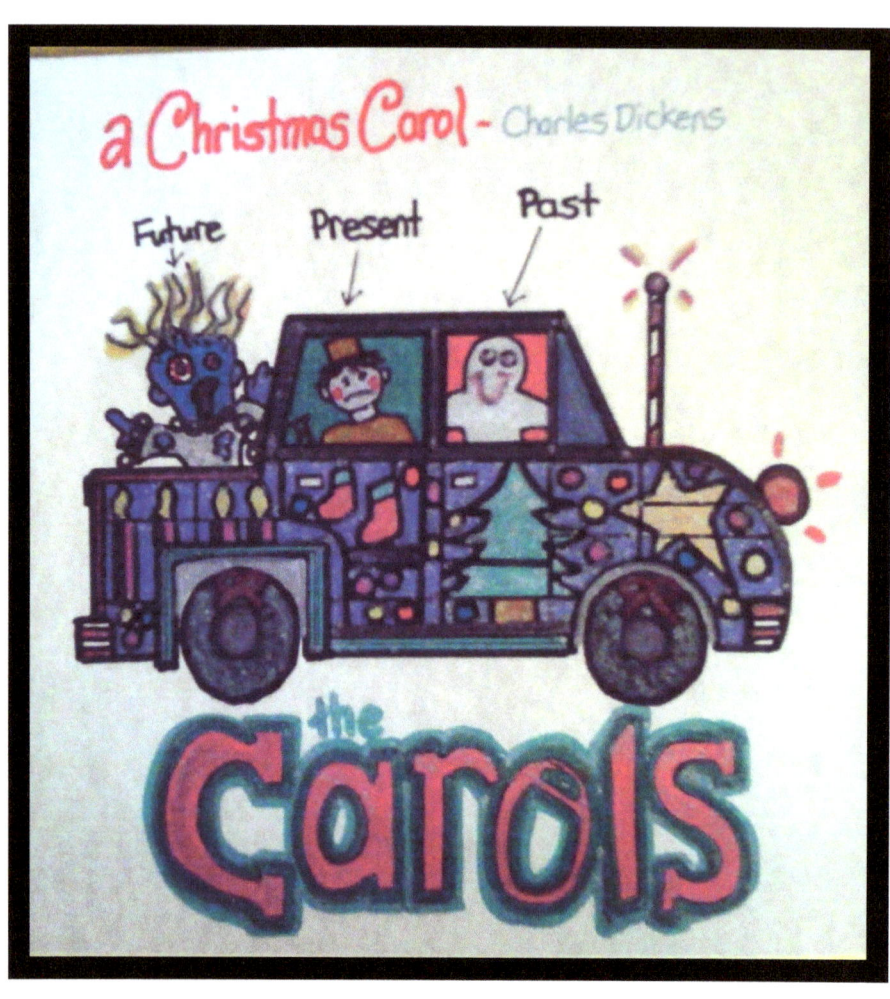

A CHRISTMAS CAROL

Kurt vonnegut jr.

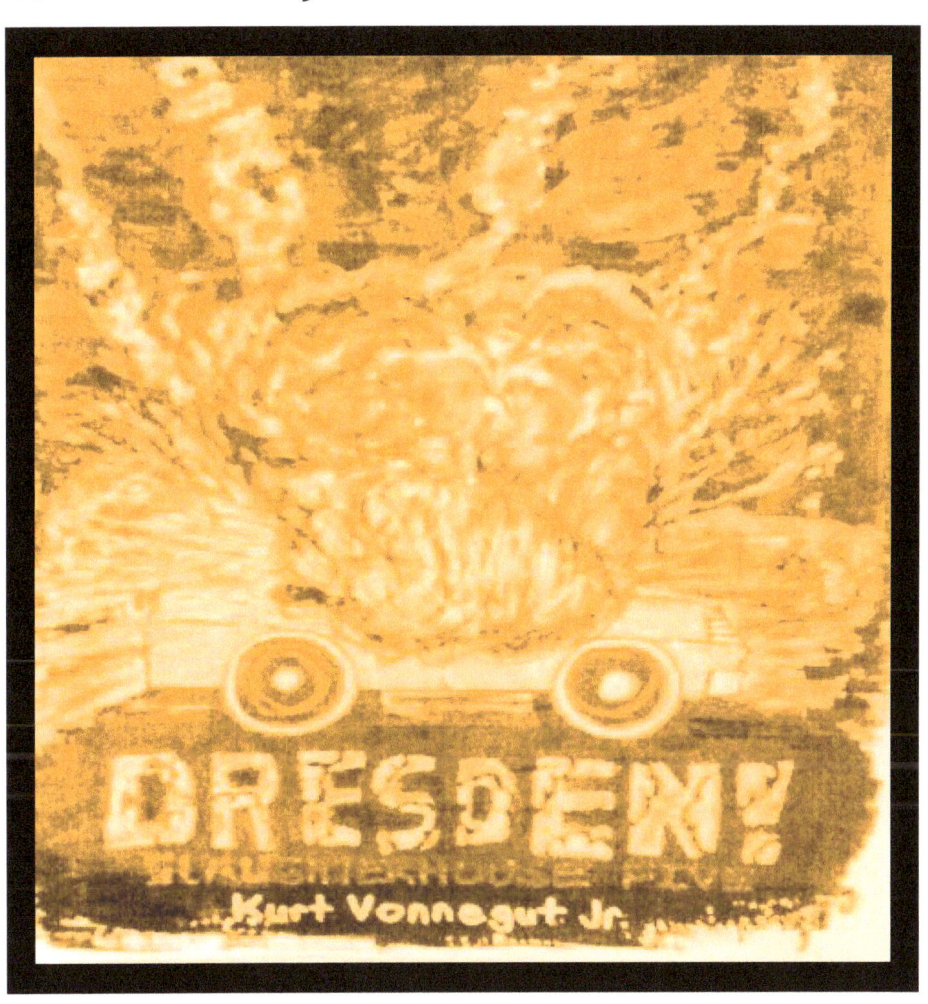

Slaughterhouse 5

Herman melville

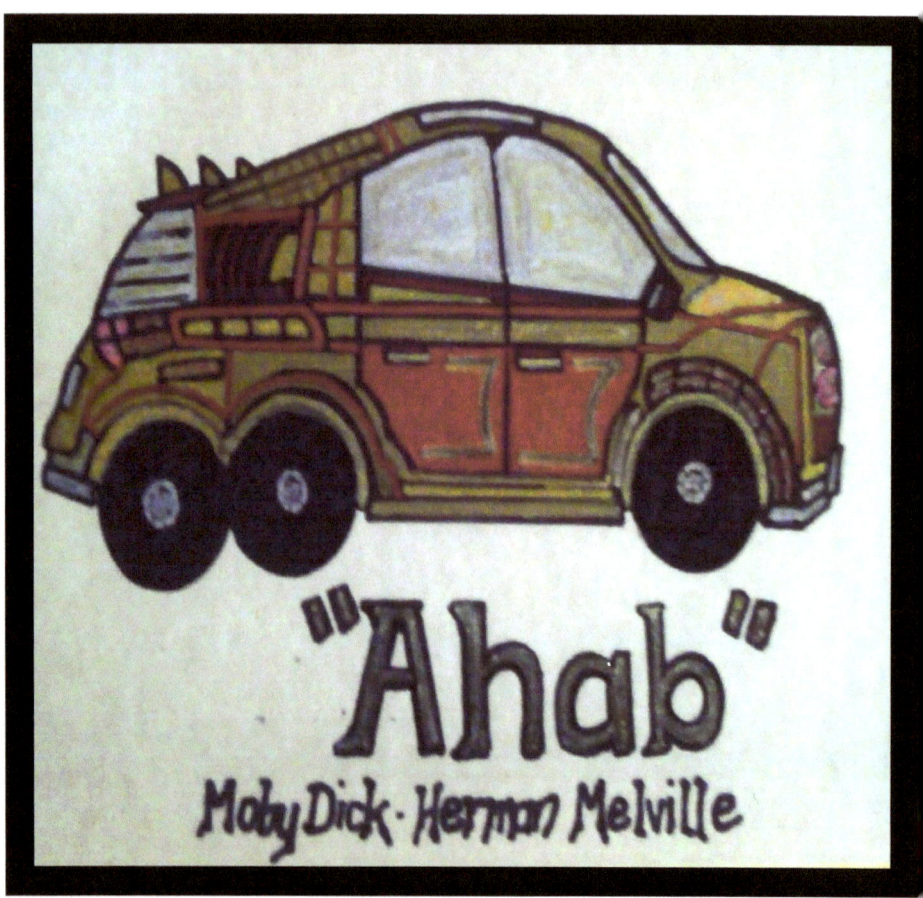

Moby dick

Edgar allan poe

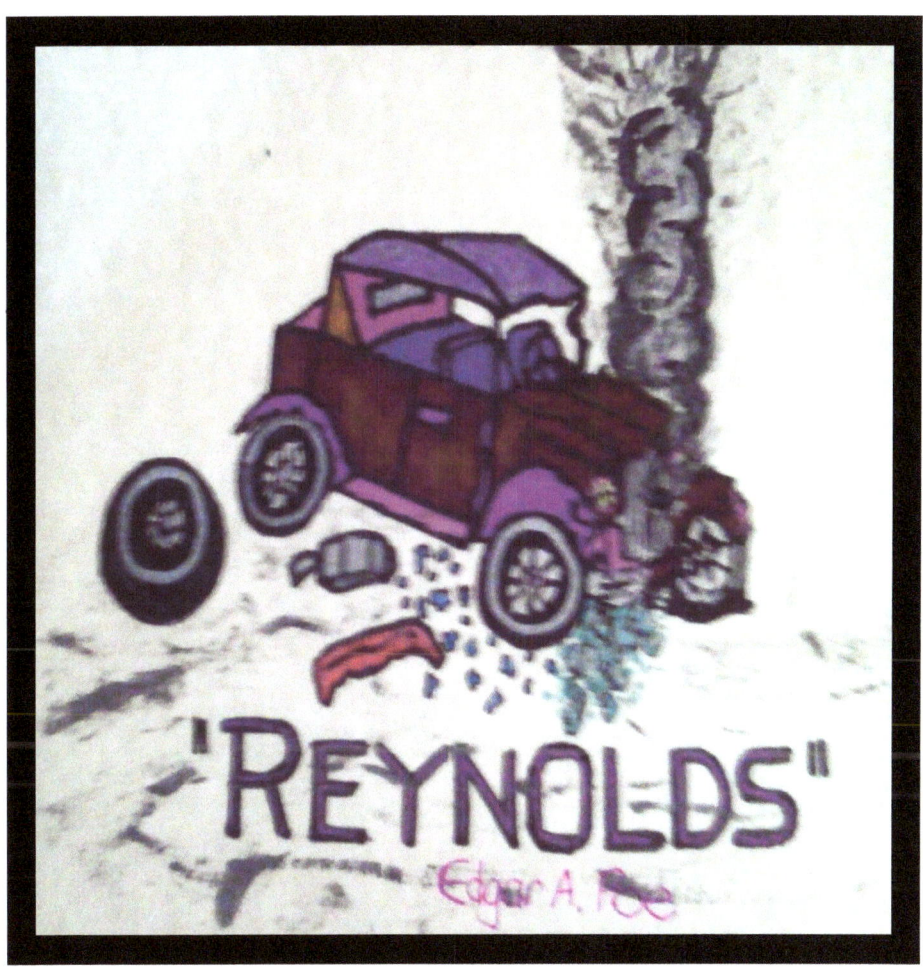

(his very last word)

Rudyard kipling

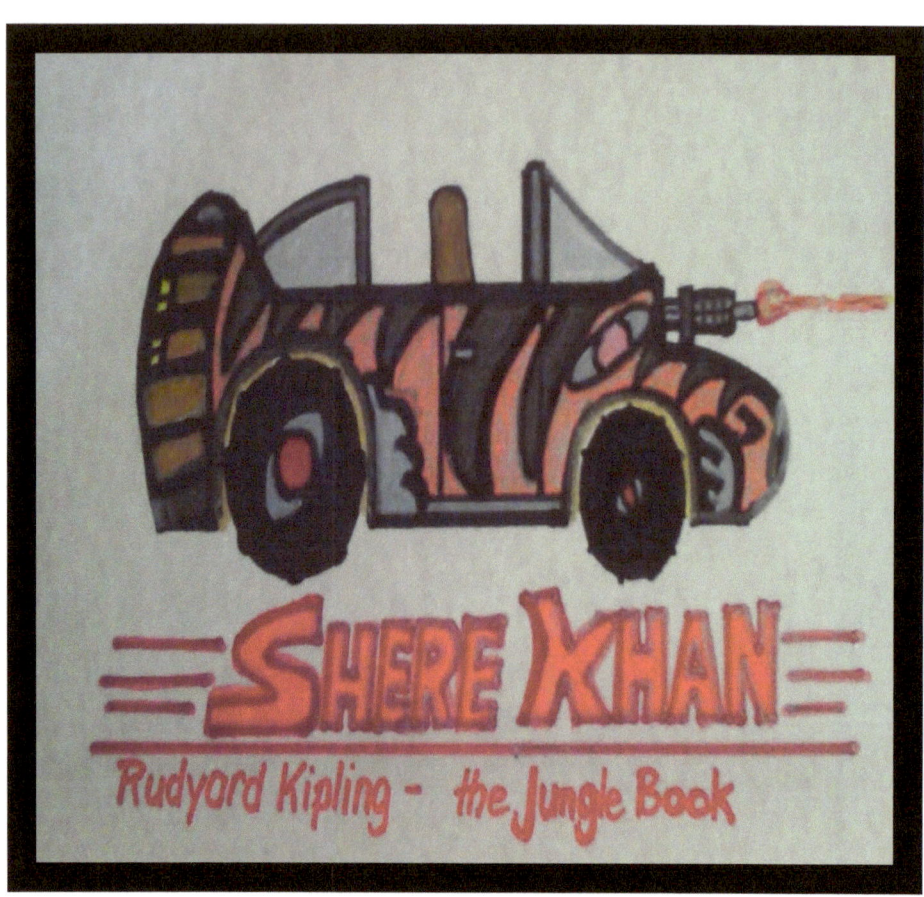

The jungle book

Sir arthur conan doyle

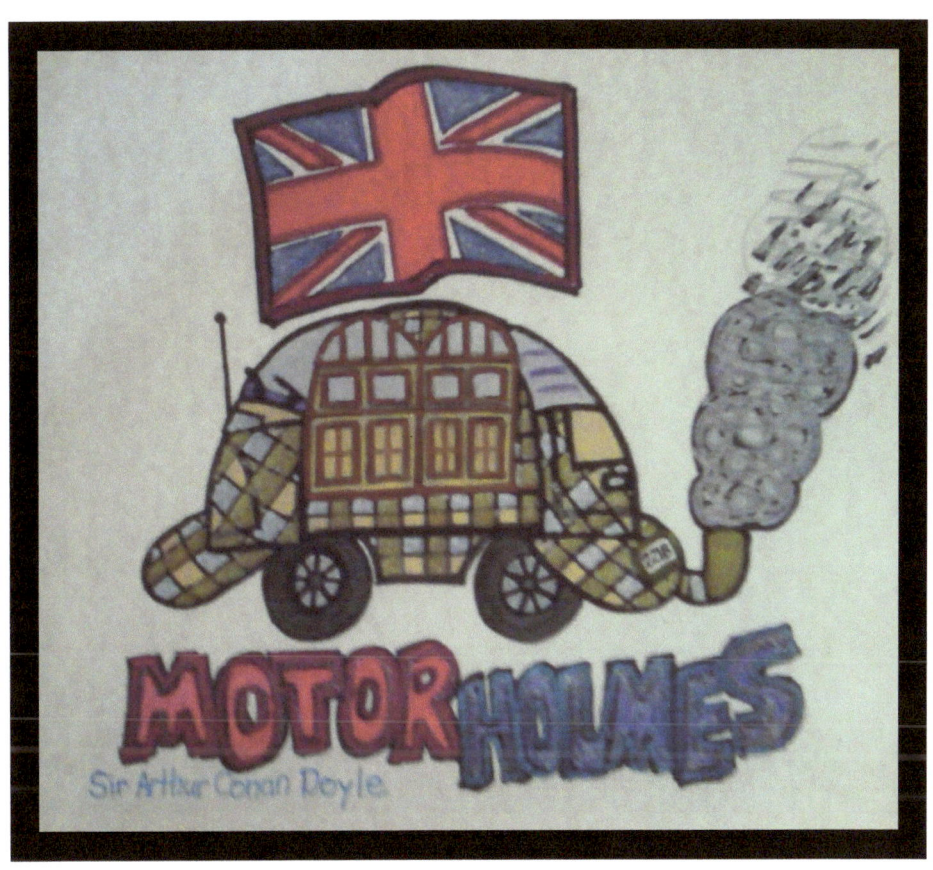

The sherlock holmes series

The end

www.ingramcontent.com/pod-product-compliance
Lightning Source LLC
Chambersburg PA
CBHW040311220526

45473CB00002B/633